ABC's of Palestine

FOR ACTIVISTS BIG AND SMALL

Created by Alia Dada

Prolance

California, USA
www.prolancewriting.com
© 2024 Alia Dada

All rights reserved. No part of the publication may be reproduced in any form without prior permission from the publisher.

979-8-9899703-0-8

Special thanks to the talented illustrators who donated art for our children and the people of Palestine.

Ayah Sadeq
(@ayah_haya)

Sama Wareh
(@thelegendofredwoodraven)

Bushra Taslim Hussain
(@islamicbeginnings)

Maimoona Shafi
(@moon_fairy_)

Salsabila Ghaisani
(@salsaghsn)

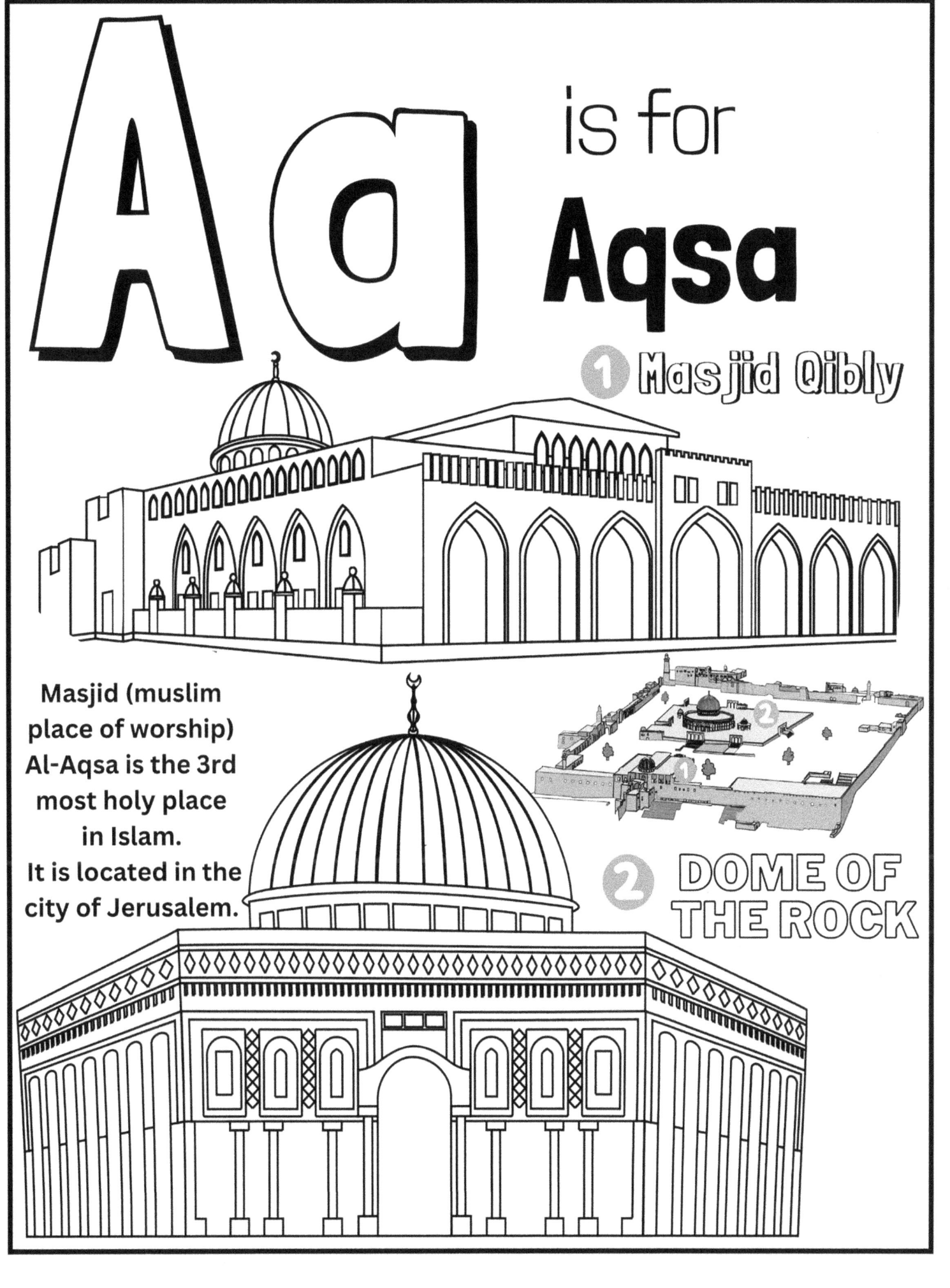

Bb is for Boycott

Boycott means to stop buying products from companies and stores that help Israel.

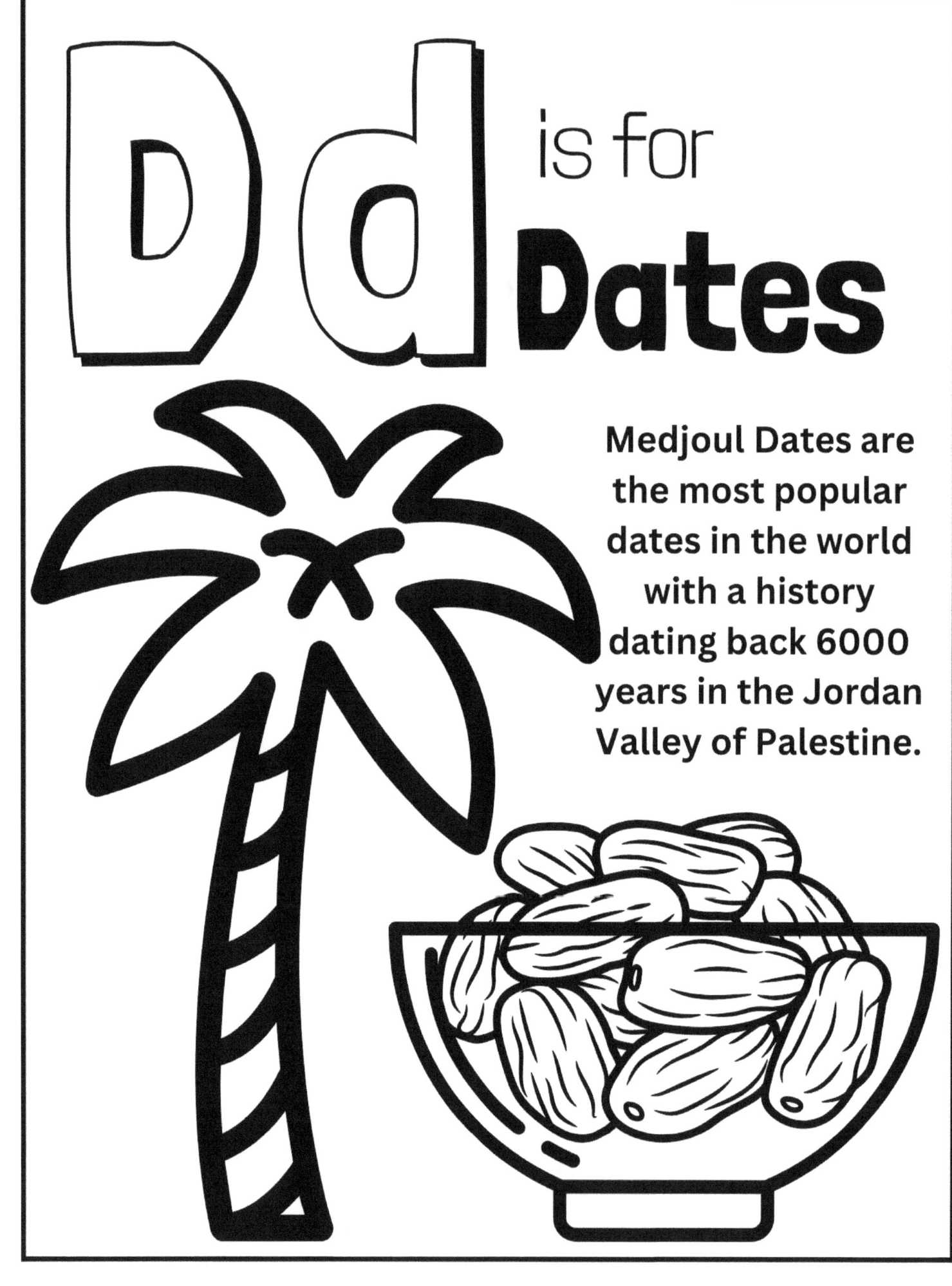

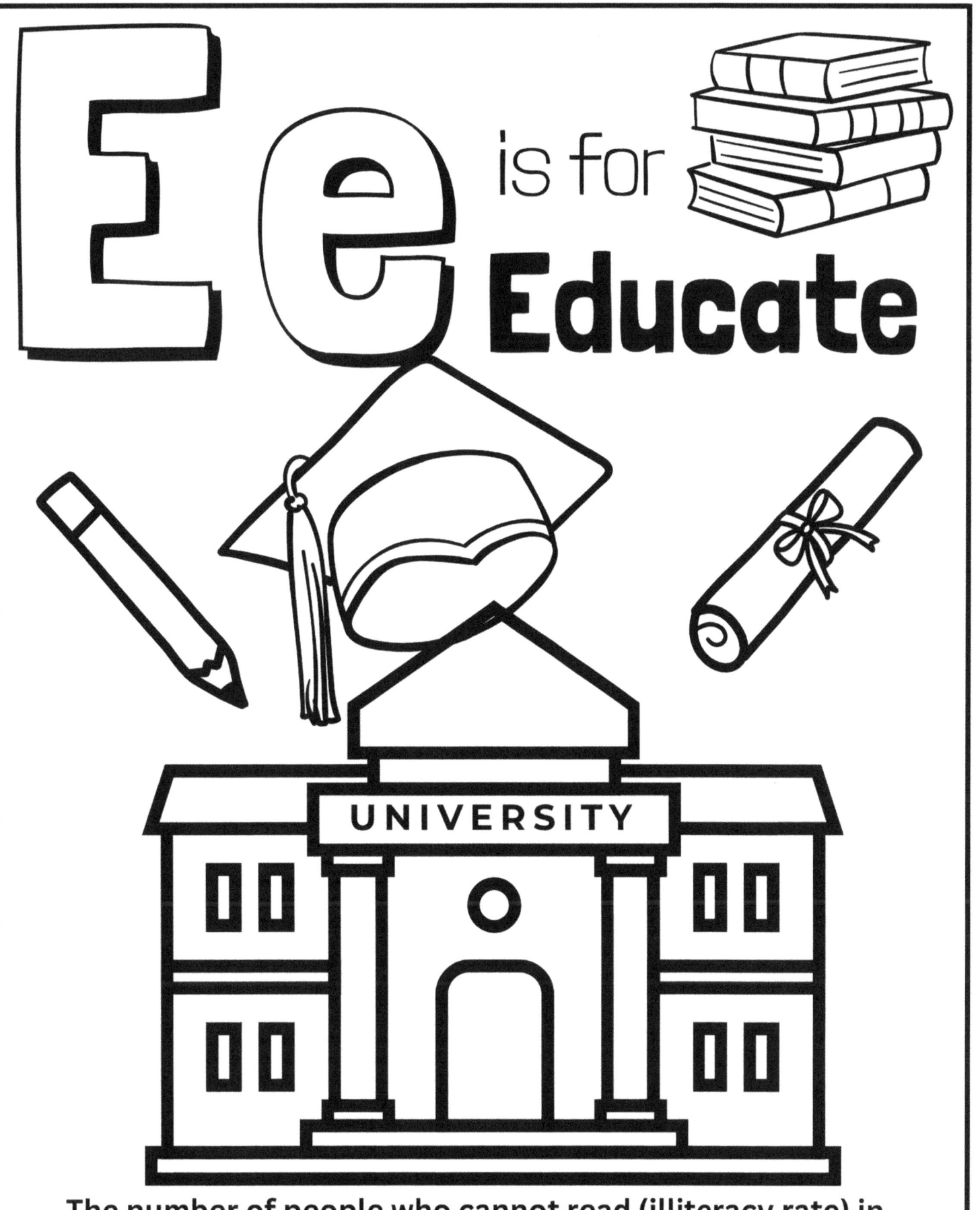

Ee is for Educate

The number of people who cannot read (illiteracy rate) in Palestine is one of the lowest in the world for Palestinians 15 years old and above in 2022.

Ff
is for
Filisteen

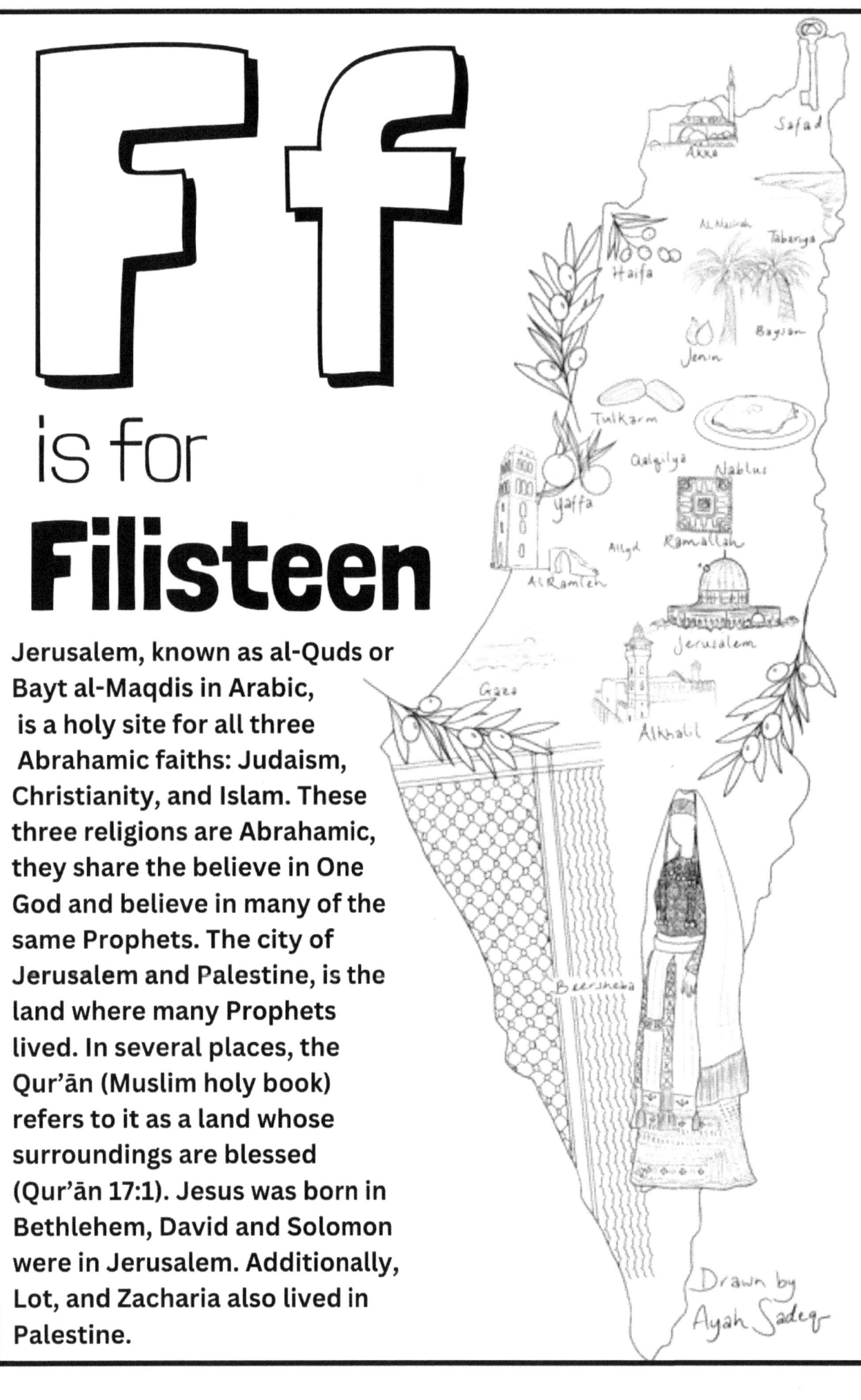

Jerusalem, known as al-Quds or Bayt al-Maqdis in Arabic, is a holy site for all three Abrahamic faiths: Judaism, Christianity, and Islam. These three religions are Abrahamic, they share the believe in One God and believe in many of the same Prophets. The city of Jerusalem and Palestine, is the land where many Prophets lived. In several places, the Qur'ān (Muslim holy book) refers to it as a land whose surroundings are blessed (Qur'ān 17:1). Jesus was born in Bethlehem, David and Solomon were in Jerusalem. Additionally, Lot, and Zacharia also lived in Palestine.

Drawn by Ayah Sadeq

Hh is for Handala

The character was created in 1969 by cartoonist Naji al-Ali. Handala remains a symbol of Palestinian identity and defiance. The name comes from Arabic: حنظل, Ḥanẓal- a plant local to Palestine which bears a bitter fruit, grows back when cut and has deep roots.

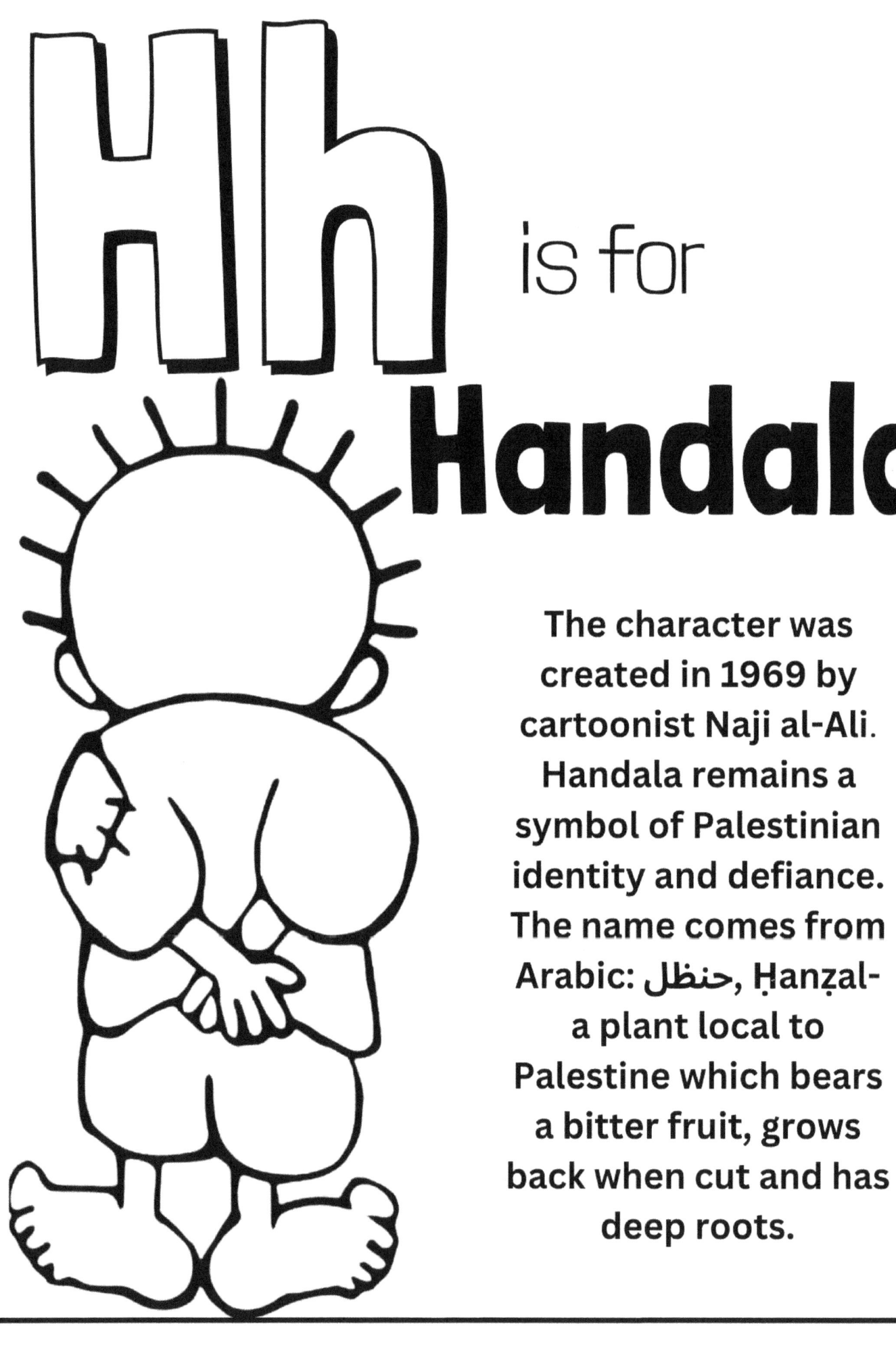

Ii is for Intifada

Meaning the Palestinians defend themselves against the Israeli military occupation of the West Bank and Gaza Strip.

The First Palestinian Intifada was in Gaza in 1987. The second in 2000.

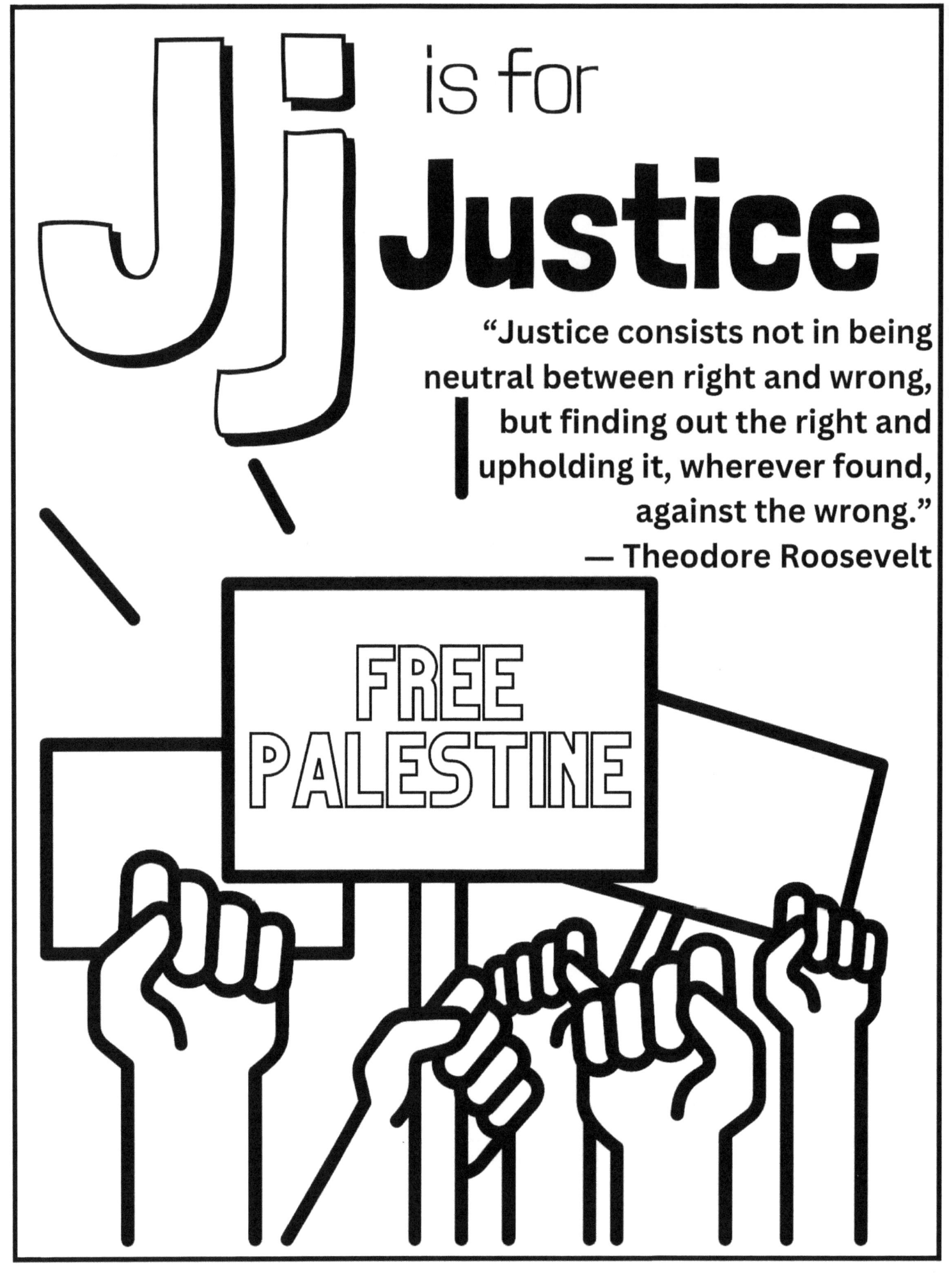

Kk is for Keffiyeh

The traditional black and white scarf Palestinians wear.

The bold pattern represents trade routes with neighboring merchants of Palestine.

The fishnet pattern represents Palestinian fishers and the people's connection to the Mediterranean.

Drawn by Ayah Sadeq

The olive-leaves pattern represents perseverance, strength and resilience.

L l is for Levant

The Levant is a geographic region that has been a center of civilization for thousands of years. It includes the countries of Jordan, Lebanon, Palestine, and Syria. Some include Iraq, Greece, Egypt, and Turkey.

Qq is for Qur'an

There are about 50,000 huffaz, people who have memorized the Qur'an (Muslim holy book), in Gaza.

Tt is for Tatreez

Tatreez is an arabic word, representing an embroidery style that is uniquely Palestinian, and dates back 3,000 years. It is a traditional form of counted needlework that uses crossed stitches and repeating motifs to tell a story. Tatreez is typically done by women, with techniques passed down through the generations and varies by region. Gaza is known for its repetition of the cypress tree motif. Ramallah is known for its use of bright and deep red thread color.

Xx is for 500x's the reward

Muslims believe every prayer offered in Masjid Al Aqsa is 500 times more rewards than any other prayer.

Zz is for Zaatar

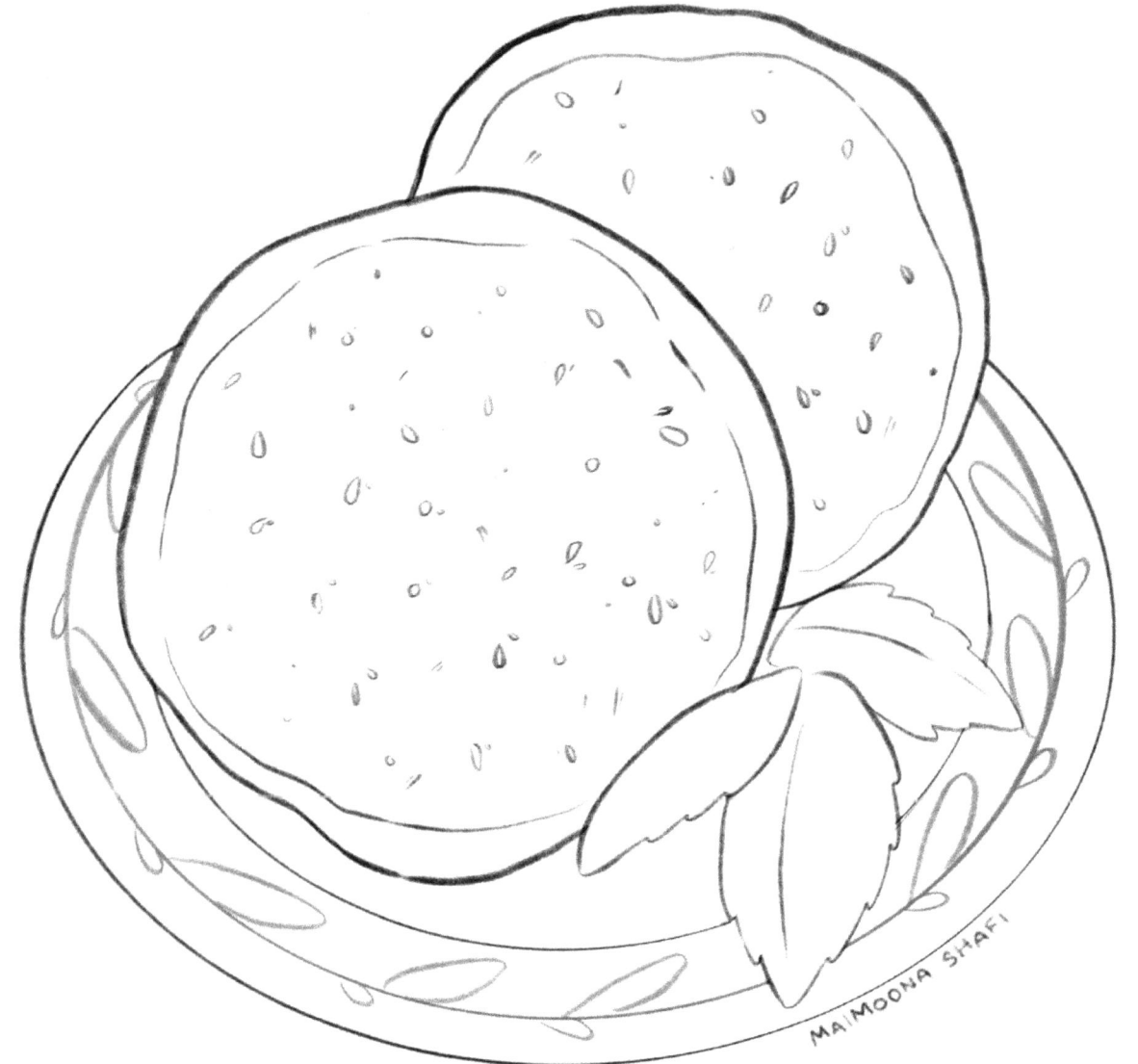

Zaatar is the Arabic name for the indigenous herb "wild thyme or oregano," but also the blend of herbs and spices. Zaatar is traditionally eaten for breakfast with pita bread and olive oil, as a topping on Manakeesh (Mana'eesh) with or without cheese, or with labne (kefir) and even on chicken!

www.ingramcontent.com/pod-product-compliance
Lightning Source LLC
Chambersburg PA
CBHW041633040426
42446CB00024B/3496